SACRED SECRETS

Living in a
State of Grace

NANI LAWRENCE, RN, MSN, CIQM

BALBOA.
PRESS
A DIVISION OF HAY HOUSE

Balboa Press books may be ordered through booksellers or by contacting:

Balboa Press A Division of Hay House 1663 Liberty Drive Bloomington, IN 47403 www.balboapress.com 1 (877) 407-4847

Because of the dynamic nature of the Internet, any web addresses or links contained in this book may have changed since publication and may no longer be valid. The views expressed in this work are solely those of the author and do not necessarily reflect the views of the publisher, and the publisher hereby disclaims any responsibility for them.

The author of this book does not dispense medical advice or prescribe the use of any technique as a form of treatment for physical, emotional, or medical problems without the advice of a physician, either directly or indirectly. The intent of the author is only to offer information of a general nature to help you in your quest for emotional and spiritual well-being. In the event you use any of the information in this book for yourself, which is your constitutional right, the author and the publisher assume no responsibility for your actions.

Cover art by Teri Vereb (www.designsbyteri.com).

Illustrations by Nani Lawrence.

Photo by Sarah Golonka (www.smg-photography.com).

Print information available on the last page.

ISBN: 978-1-5043-9708-7 (sc) ISBN: 978-1-5043-9710-0 (hc)
ISBN: 978-1-5043-9709-4 (e)

Library of Congress Control Number: 2018901488

Balboa Press rev. date: 02/27/2018

To Louise Mita, without whom my life could not have catapulted to these heights. You offered me the tools to open the Pandora's box of my soul and do some major spring cleaning. In the process of clearing out antiquated beliefs, mysterious misconceptions, and a bevy of psychic dust bunnies, these sacred secrets were uncovered. *Mahalo ke akua* ...

To my children, Bud, Déja, Amira, Alana, and Jordan: You (and your families) are the reason why this work is so important to me. I can only imagine how awkward it must be to have a mother who is an unconventional healer, converses with invisible beings, and can make magic happen with the snap of her fingers. Thank you for your undying support of my epic weirdness! I love you to the moon and beyond.

Special thanks to Teri Vereb, whose spiritually inspired cover art, including the stunning and magical Goddess Ilona, is a testament to the gifts and talents of this amazing artist, a tribute to our infinite lifetimes as soul sisters, and a commitment to the promulgation of sacred secrets everywhere.

Mahalo nui loa to Andrea Smith for her heartfelt introduction (see Foreword), her eternal friendship, her visionary art, and her ancient wisdom. My heart is full, knowing that there is so much joy to share, as we travel to the ends of the Earth, igniting one heart at a time in our quest for peace.

FOREWORD

Andrea Smith, Artist/ Visionary/Activist for Peace

I have known Nani Lawrence for thirty-six years. She was a gorgeous young woman with a cascade of dark curls down her brown, tanned back when I first met her on Maui in 1982, and she always had one of her blonde babies hanging on her hip. They were all beautiful and looked like locals. Nani had a calming presence – her voice was soft and wise. I felt very connected to her from the moment I met her and was inspired to create an angelic painting about her daughter, Amira.

I was busy with my career and family, and she had her hands full. Over time, we lost touch. That is, until social media allowed us to reconnect years later when we were both more available. I fell in love with Nani all over again! This Nani is a very wise, assured and grown woman! Her entire being is filled with grace.

After nearly thirty years, we reunited in-person in Egypt! My husband and I take groups to various power spots on the planet, and Nani joined us on such a trip in 2017. In front of me was a beautiful woman who had blossomed into a loving sage! All her trials and tribulations had transformed her into a being of light!

We can either hold onto our hurts or grow from them. When we let go, we are rewarded with incredible gifts and blessings that are hard to imagine unless we do it. Well, she has gone through the fire and come out purified. She has faced herself, gone within, and seen only the love. In reality, that is who she always was, but she is such a love-filled being, it probably took time and five children to really embrace it.

Sacred Secrets is a very personal story of what growth, determination, and destiny can accomplish. I think often about someone like Nani in the nursing profession, with her energy and sweetness, showing up when people are at their most vulnerable. It's a better planet because my precious friend is on it, and I get to share the experience with her!

God is good!

Andrea Smith
February 7, 2018

NOTE

This story contains vignettes from my own personal experiences that do not always appear in chronological (or logical) order. The examples that are offered are meant to illustrate the topic discussed in the chapter. Allow yourself to flow with the story rather than trying to make sense of my life, which I'm not entirely sure is possible!

CONTENTS

PROLOGUE

A Reflection from My Older Self

Cast as the main character in each captivating chapter of my fairy tale life, I have been the beneficiary of many *sacred secrets* that have collectively evolved into a deeply transformative and timely message. Now is the perfect moment for me to share these gems through my story.

This multidimensional tale is not only one of wisdom but of beauty. There have been lessons learned, changes spun into motion, and truths told in the process of these secrets being revealed. The plethora of puzzle pieces I've gathered along my journey through life have seamlessly interlocked to form an exquisite masterpiece, allowing me to *master peace*.

At the crossroads where I stand at this moment, there are no regrets. I am eternally grateful for each unique opportunity that led me here. Most were not chosen *by* me but *for* me. I was pushed out of my comfort zone, sent off on adventures of discovery (both internal and external), and exposed to experiences I could never have dreamed possible.

My path has been arduous and unpredictable but ultimately rewarding. I am blessed beyond belief to have become the most genuine version of me. My inner child is joyful. My temple resides within. My religion is kindness. I take delight in inspiring others to uncover their truth, and my purest intention is to make this world a better place for future generations.

My good friend, internationally renowned artist and activist for peace Andrea Smith, expressed this concept to me in a recent conversation: From the moment we are born, our lifetime experiences make up a unique soup that contains the essence of who we will become. Throughout our lives, we chase our dreams with enthusiasm, savor our choices with passion, marinate each event in emotions, and relish our intimate moments with others. These experiences and feelings are stirred into the soup. Over the years, the soup simmers down to a rich, full-bodied stew as we evolve toward perfection. At the end of our lives, all that is left is our pure essence. The key is to choose our ingredients well. Here is my recipe.

1

Being Fearless

Having courage does not mean that we are unafraid.—*Maya Angelou*

This empowering story was inspired early one morning at 4:44 a.m. I was abruptly awakened with a strong intuitive understanding that the most powerful and fearless human I can be is not someone with superpowers or with magically activated protective armor but the person I am when aligned with the core of my being. When I connect with my higher self and innate wisdom—which is accessible to me when I am centered and grounded—I am fearless and impervious to anything that might otherwise scare the crap out of me.

I knew I was empathic at an early age. Empaths are sensitive to what is going on around them, perceiving what some people are thinking and sensing what others are feeling. They are intuitively aware, meaning that they know things without having thought of them. My younger self interpreted this sensitivity as something to fear—not realizing that it was, in fact, a gift.

Growing up this way was scary. No one understood me, and I always felt alone. I was introverted and shy. Everything appeared larger than life and insurmountable. As an adolescent, I learned to approach circumstances much like a chameleon, saying what people wanted to hear and doing what was expected of me. This was the genesis of a survival-based belief that if I wanted to succeed in life, I needed to compromise my body, my values, and my integrity. I was selling myself out.

Navigating through life in this way is terrifying. We play a game that we can't win. When we lie to ourselves or anyone else, we are telling a story and putting on an award-winning act. There end up being a lot of stories to remember, and we can get a little defensive or maybe even frightened about being caught in them. There are a lot of not-very-nice people out there, so some of us find it easier to be compliant with their agendas as we fearfully maneuver through life.

It always amazed me, as an Emergency Nurse, that many women who came in battered, beaten, or raped by their domestic partners declined to file police reports, refused to go to safe houses, and demanded to be discharged back home after treatment. When reminded that their next visit to the hospital might be to the morgue in a body bag, they insisted that they were increasing the likelihood of certain death by not showing up at home in a timely manner. Fear is an unforgiving master.

When we live life in this way, we lose track of our identity and true purpose. On our journey toward the Garden of Future Successes, we can inadvertently end up in the Swamp of Past Failures. The harder we work to prove who we think we need to be, the less we resemble the person we really are. Therefore, some of us feel like we are lonely when we're clearly not alone. This is because we are missing ourselves.

When we are true to ourselves, we don't have to remember such stories - at any given moment, we're simply being honest. It takes courage to stand up in an intimidating scenario and say, "No, that doesn't work for me." But by doing this, we are saying *yes* to ourselves, advocating for our values, and defending our integrity.

If there is fear in being autonomous, rising up to speak our truths, or walking away from uncomfortable situations, there is exponentially more fear in allowing ourselves to be bullied, ignored, abused, or forced into submission. With practice, we discover that being our own champion engenders respect from others. It is also incredibly empowering, because we learn to value ourselves in the process—especially when there are risks or obstacles to overcome.

Les Brown observed, "Too many of us are not living our dreams because we are living our fears." Two years ago, I had an epiphany along those lines. I had spent most of my life trapped in a Fortress of Fear, built out of limiting beliefs that no longer served me, especially the ones that minimized my self-worth. There had been several opportunities for me to escape over the years, yet I swiftly sabotaged those attempts with my insecure, self-defeating behavior. I convinced myself that I was thriving in this self-imposed enclave, deluded as I was by the false sense of security that it afforded me. Aware that this fortress had a door, I finally realized that I'd had the key in my possession all along. One day not long ago, I was ready to let myself out.

My first few experiences of being fearless inspired me so profoundly that I might have done a happy dance or two! One of these moments occurred when I declined a prominent role in the health care profession because the expectations that went with it clearly violated my personal values. I was so proud to honor myself in this way, as if I had produced a priceless work of art and was now unveiling it to the world. The work of art was me!

2

Being Protected

The most glorious moment you will ever experience in your life is when you look back and see how God was protecting you all this time.—Shannon L. Alder

I was raised without strong religious or spiritual influences, given that my father had lost his faith in God by the time he graduated college. Yet I always believed in a greater power and experienced a profound sense of protection that was omnipresent. It was not my family, friends, or teachers who sheltered me from harm as a child and adolescent, but rather a mysteriously pervasive supernatural force that remained invisible to me for decades.

Throughout my life, I have been intuitively compelled to change course on what seemed like well-planned routes. In my younger, more rebellious years, I did not always heed these urgings of my conscience, having no idea what those annoying thoughts were or where they came from. Instead, I stubbornly chose to keep my unwavering commitment to the plan or task at hand, often resulting in unfavorable outcomes.

I decided to take a backpacking trip to the island of Kaua'i in 1974 and hitchhiked to the North Shore with my year-old son, Bud, in tow. After spending the night camping at Ke'e Beach, I hiked two miles along the Kalalau Trail and set up camp at Hanakāpī'ai Beach. This is an awe-inspiring open-water bay with a pristine beach. Hiking farther into the Hanakāpī'ai Valley, I discovered a majestic three-hundred-foot waterfall that was breathtaking to behold. I decided this remote paradise would be our home for a couple of days.

The next morning, while bodysurfing in the cold and rather rough waves, I lost my great-grandmother's engagement ring. My mom had passed this family heirloom along to me when I graduated high school and it had not left my finger since. Now, in an instant, it slipped off into the deep blue surf, never to be seen again. I took it as a sign that maybe we should head back out of the valley that same day, warning that this was a minor loss, but something worse might be at stake. But I chose to ignore the sign, as I had originally planned to spend one more night.

A tropical storm hit the North Shore the following day. Everyone in the encampment was taking down tents and rushing to hike out while it was still possible, so I followed suit. With Bud in a baby carrier strapped to the front of me and a thirty-pound pack on my back, I tried to make my way through floodwater that had turned a simple stream into a raging river. I slipped on the mossy rocks midstream, and we fell into the rushing water. We would have been swept away if not for a couple of campers who grabbed my pack and helped us safely to the other side of the stream.

While hiking the remainder of the two miles in torrential rain, the muddy edge of the mountainside trail suddenly gave way beneath my feet. Again, the quick reaction of fellow hikers saved us from sliding down the two-hundred-foot cliff into the sea below. There is no question that we were being protected, yet it would have been far less dangerous to have left before the storm.

Soon after, I put two and two together and got a clue. I learned to be attentive to those silent but clear messages. And when I did - you guessed it - the outcomes dramatically improved. I now acknowledge this guidance as a spiritual GPS, if you will, and eagerly engage in a method of accessing this wisdom to direct me safely along my path.

In February of 1980, with three small children, I leased a home on the Big Island of Hawai'i. The repurposed wooden coffeehouse stood on the slopes of Captain Cook with a panorama overlooking Kealakekua Bay. In late November, I felt a strong, sudden urge to leave the island, but it was more of an undeniable sense of impending doom. Without understanding why, I instinctively knew that I had less than a week to pack up our things and leave.

My lease wasn't due to expire until February of the following year, but the landlady was understanding when I explained that I felt an urgent need to leave the island immediately. I made plans for us to move back to the island of Oahu the day after Thanksgiving. To lighten our load, we gifted many of our belongings to others in our community, and I sold my car to cover the cost of travel expenses. Our friends hosted a going-away party for us over a bountiful Thanksgiving dinner, and we left the island hastily Friday morning.

Our gracious host, Kaveri, called on Saturday afternoon to inquire as to how we were settling in on Oahu. Her voice wavered as she mentioned that it was a stroke of luck that we had managed to get out the house when we did. "Why?" I asked. She informed me that our house had burned down to the ground at around three o'clock that morning. The fire had been caused by an electrical malfunction in the kitchen downstairs. The bedrooms were all located on the top floor. I took a deep breath and felt overwhelmingly grateful for the guidance I had received a week earlier.

There are no coincidences. This is one thing of which I am certain.

I understand now that there are many sacred souls who watch over me. In earlier years, I referred to them as my spirit guides. They are ascendant beings representing a collective conscious source energy, protecting me from harm and always encouraging me to become the most amazing version of myself. Their messages are transmitted vibrationally, though I interpret these intuitive feelings or visions into words to better make sense of this information or to be able to share their wisdom with others. Occasionally, they show up in human form to prompt me to continue moving in a purposeful direction.

Three weeks after I had given my notice of resignation from my career as an Emergency Department Manager in Northern California (fast-forward to 2015), I suddenly became a bit remorseful about my decision to leave the ER to become a bedside Hospice nurse - a choice I was guided to make. This was likely an emotional response to the sadness and disappointment that my employees and colleagues expressed over my impending departure – but may have had a little to do with the fifty percent cut in pay.

One evening, with just a few more days left in the Emergency Department, a nurse asked me to go to

Room 14 and speak with the family there. I requested a backstory—as I was frequently called to intervene with patient/family issues—but the nurse explained that the patient's wife was Hawaiian and, discovering that I was from Hawaii, merely wanted to *talk story* with me.

Shirley and I began chatting and we eventually ended up on the topic of how the spiritual veil between reality and alternate dimensions was significantly thinner in Hawaii than here on the Mainland. We shared several stories of our firsthand experiences of this mystical phenomenon. She and I bonded during our intensely graphic conversation.

When it came time for her husband to be discharged home, I offered her my business card, mentioning that I'd be leaving the Emergency Department at the end of the week. She asked me about my future plans, so I told her about Hospice. What came next led me to believe that Shirley was one of my spiritual guardians, a human angel sent to reassure me about my present purpose.

She whispered in a soft voice, "Despite your inner conflict over leaving here, it is of the utmost importance that you go to this new job. You cannot get where you are headed on your path from this place. Although you will not be at the new job for very long, it is your bridge to get to where you need to go on your journey."

Wait, what?

Then she asked, "Do you know what makes you special?"

"No," I replied, not sure where she was heading with this question.

"Everyone gets messages," she continued. "Not everyone hears them. Of those, very few listen to discern the meaning. And of those few, it's rare that someone acts on the messages they receive. You are one of those rare people."

How could she possibly know this?

As it turned out, I did leave my job as planned. I worked at Hospice for only seven months before being invited to take a prestigious job in Southern California. (You'll find out what happened next in chapter 4.)

It is my intuitive understanding that we *all* have spiritual guardians who protect and guide us.

3

Being Love

Love is a process of inclusion. Once I include
you as a part of me, I will be to you just
the way I am to myself.—Sadhguru

I was raised in a home where love and affection closely
resembled love letters to a blind girl. You can safely
assume that I had no resident expert to coach me in the
how-to-be-loving department. It's not that my parents
didn't love me - it's just that they didn't know how to
show it in a way that I had an experience of being loved
by them (they obviously had no experts in their own
families either).

As a young girl, I was always jealous of friends at
school who had (what appeared to be) loving relationships

with their parents. How I wished that my mom was like theirs: fun, affectionate, understanding, and most of all, available. My childhood dream, which I loosely based on these maternal role models, was to grow up to be loving, kind, compassionate, and willing to make time to listen and be present, both as a parent and as a human being.

Throughout much of my adulthood, being passionate and selfless turned out to be a one-way street, and I wasn't feeling the love in return. Although I've always considered myself an optimist, I honestly wasn't any happier than I had been as a young girl or adolescent. It wasn't until I was almost sixty years old that I had a revelation about how love works.

To illustrate my aha moment, imagine me carrying around a Love Cup. It already had some love in it, but I generously kept giving the love away. For years I traveled the world, searching for whomever might be lucky enough to fill up my cup, but it never even got close to full. My lengthy list of uneventful relationships even included a few short-term marriages. In retrospect, the common denominator in these lackluster liaisons was *me*. I never chose a partner who could love me in a way that I had an experience of being loved by them.

After years of asking myself what I was doing wrong, I decided to ask, "What can I do differently?" I discovered that the answer was simple: search for love within or, simply, fall in love with myself. *Oh! Okay!* Slowly but surely, the love in the cup began to swell. To my delight, my Love Cup is now overflowing with enchanting effervescence, and I'm always looking for others to share it with because the supply of unconditional love is endless. *Aha!*

Gerald Jampolsky adds this auspicious advice to the equation: "If you don't forgive your mother and father, all of your partners in relationships will be versions of your mother and father." This realization was pivotal for me, inspiring me to relinquish the anger I'd been harboring toward my mother *forever.* After all, it wasn't her fault that I hadn't felt loved. I forgave her (for never having learned how to be loving or affectionate) and myself (for blaming her and holding a grudge all these years). I wanted to take responsibility and come from a place of self-love.

The next time we went out to dinner, I was taken by surprise when my mom and I had a delightful time together. The following day, while speaking with my daughter Amira, I casually mentioned, "By the way, something strange has happened to your grandmother—she's a totally different person. I had dinner with her last night, and she was caring, funny, and charming. She even told me how proud she is of me, and I just quit my job. It's the first time I've ever enjoyed spending time with her."

Amira responded, "It has nothing to do with her, Mom. It's *you* that's changed."

In seeking to establish and enhance our deepest relationships with others, we can only offer the level of intimacy that we have achieved first with ourselves. Additionally, we can empower one another by unconditionally accepting and supporting the most vulnerable versions of ourselves and our love ones. We can also increase the odds of our relationships succeeding when we commit to give of ourselves rather than take for ourselves. The truth is, if we want to be truly happy, it's not about loving or being loved by others. It's about *being love.*

4

Being Present

Never assume that loud is strong and
quiet is weak.—Unknown

My next challenge, coming from the relatively new perspective of loving myself, was reconnecting with my authentic self or the essence of who I am. I was so immersed in my career at this point that there was zero time for the people I loved or the things I enjoyed doing, let alone time for myself. My personal life was stuck in survival mode: eat, sleep, work, eat, sleep, work.

I decided that discovering who I was—and what I love about me and my life—was an urgent priority. I also realized that if I continued working sixty hours per week, I would be headed for a health crisis. My lifestyle was not even close to sustainable. I was already experiencing significant symptoms of stress: high blood pressure, inflammatory issues, and insomnia, to name a few.

Having attempted for years to be a legendary nurse heroine with superpowers, it turned out that I was only human after all. So I quit. Let me share with you how the story unraveled.

After leaving Hospice and moving to Southern California, the prominent position I was offered never materialized. Zero. Zip. Nada. I was astonished by how I responded to this unexpected turn of events: no panic over losing my source of employment and income; no anger over being duped into leaving a secure job, giving most of my stuff away, and moving everything else four hundred miles away; no blame directed toward the person who promised me the position, encouraged me to move, and then never got back to me—ever.

I remembered what Shirley mentioned about a bridge that would take me to the next destination in my journey, and I tried to imagine if this void was exactly where I was supposed to be right now. What was my destiny, anyway? Being unemployed? I'd weirdly sensed that this job wasn't going to work out, even before I left, but I gathered that it was a sign, in which case I was being guided to make this move anyway.

I envisioned taking a few months to travel and decompress – then maybe extending the time off into a yearlong sabbatical or perhaps even considering early retirement. These were just fleeting thoughts, you understand, because I was still in a *WTF just happened?* state of shock. All I knew was that I needed a break, and now was the perfect time to take one.

I launched my new and improved lifestyle in 2016 on New Year's Day and called it my Soul Journey, an adventure dedicated to personal exploration. The first several months were the most uncomfortable, as I encountered an unanticipated withdrawal process. Having once excelled at being a professional problem-solver an multitasker, I found myself making a valiant effort to sit still and, well, just *be* still. Not knowing how to diffuse my intellectual energy, I was literally vibrating for hours on end.

I was intrigued to learn that the word *listen* contains the exact same letters as the word *silent*. I began to experiment with being a better listener, since I was no longer compelled to justify my existence or prove my self-worth in a corporate environment. And don't let anyone tell you otherwise: listening is a skill that requires practice, patience, and commitment.

The more I listened, the more I realized that others don't. My mom used to drive me nuts by asking me a question and then, before I was halfway through my response, verbalizing her next thought. *Not okay!* So now I make the effort to really hear what someone is saying, because if I'm listening to reply, I'm not listening to understand.

I also sense how truly therapeutic it is when others feel that they are being heard and their concerns are acknowledged. Referring to some of their main talking points lets them know that I hear and validate their concerns. When my son-in-law Brian says, "I can't believe the car *still* isn't running right," I might respond by saying, "I can tell you're really frustrated about the car." This is a simple acknowledgment that I understand his dilemma.

I found myself making a practice of *holding space* for others—being quiet, listening, and not judging. I accept their viewpoint for what it is, without questioning their position or feeling the need to defend mine. Sometimes I'll ask questions if I need to better understand a perspective that differs from mine. *Who knows*, I say to myself, *maybe I'll learn something that causes me to redefine my reality*. And on occasion, I do.

The Dalai Lama states, "When you talk, you are only repeating what you already know. But if you listen, you may learn something new." Whenever I have the urge to share my opinions on a topic, I remind myself that they don't really matter to anyone else but me. After all, it is my actions that are the strongest statements of what I believe. However, if I'm in a situation where my input is requested (such as a meeting), I've learned to wait until everyone else has had a chance to address concerns on the subject. Their comments inform and influence my response.

What has become most important to me, in every interaction or conversation I'm having with myself or others, is that I choose to show up and be present. Otherwise, it's as if I'm skimming through a book without really reading it. Making a priority of being fully engaged in this manner has been a game-changer in all my relationships.

I meditate (sit or lay still and listen) anywhere from a few minutes to an hour each day. This allows me to hold space for and honor my inner or higher self. I receive some of my most life-directing intuitive messages during these times. These mindful moments also give me opportunities to send loving thoughts or healing prayers to those who are struggling, especially those with whom I don't see eye to eye. This is one of the ways in which I share my overflowing love, from a place of pure humility.

I spend more time outside, embracing the wisdom and magnificence of Mother Nature. Being near the ocean or in the mountains (which I'm fortunate to have close by) is incredibly peaceful and powerful for me, especially if I choose to leave my electronic devices tucked away. Nature restores my energetic balance and soothes my soul.

Sometimes I take a random road trip or wander into my community without a set purpose in mind, just to remove myself from the demands of my personal agenda and expose myself to an external reality. It takes the burden of responsibility off me, however briefly, and allows me to appreciate my essential freedom of being. As I become more present, I notice more of what's going on around me. To some, these may seem like trivial things. I watched an owl perching on the oak tree in my backyard; a mother dropping her keys at the market while trying to comfort her crying baby; a homeless man sitting on the sidewalk hoping for a handout. Amazing things show up when we do.

Engaging in these experiences allows me to be more responsive to the needs of others rather than just focusing on my own. I sent the owl some virtual love, picked up the keys for that mom (and helped carry the groceries to her car), and offered my doggy bag of leftover lunch to the homeless man. These altruistic opportunities are commonly referred to as *random acts of kindness*. They connect us to a shared experience of humanity. By being present and making someone else's day, I make mine better as well.

5

Being Able to Choose

You're always one decision away from a
totally different life.—Mark Batterson

Things rarely go as planned. For a moment, bear with me
and consider this: What if we gave up all expectations?
We would never be disappointed, frustrated, or angry,
right? We would be choosing to go with the flow instead
of always trying to swim upstream (and believe me,
nothing we are searching for is upstream anyway). Well,
since my career departure suddenly shifted the course
of the stream I was in, I've been learning how to float
downstream.

This is about choice. We all have free will, or the
ability to choose between different courses of action. But

when we make such a choice, we are opening ourselves up to criticism. Been there. Done that. For as long as I can remember, I had a starring role as my own worst critic. And then it seemed everyone else also had an opinion about what I was up to.

In the past, I felt the responsibility of wanting to do what was right for everyone else and the guilt of not being able to make everyone's day. At this point in my life, I care less about others judging what I do and more about being true to myself and following my heart. Everything in our lives reflects the choices we make. If we want different results, we need to choose differently.

Something worth mentioning here is how we influence those we care most about. Some of us tend to be rescuers or enablers. I have given away thousands of dollars (not to mention my time and energy) in various efforts to help family and friends get their act together. I thought it was my job to save my loved ones from every risky choice or dire situation. Ironically, it *was* my real job as an Emergency Department Nurse and Manager, but I'm not talking about those kinds of emergencies here.

I was proud to be a philanthropist in this way, donating to everyone else's personal charity, frequently at the expense of not meeting my own needs. Often, those I "rescued" would repeatedly ask for assistance while neglecting to make any effort to change their risky behaviors or otherwise extricate themselves from their hopeless situations.

It's important to realize that we can't force others to change their behavior. Only they can facilitate their own transformation and find fulfillment in this world. It's a harsh reality, especially if we're enablers. I've come to this conclusion: if others have a life lesson to learn or karma to work out by overcoming a challenging situation, why should I deprive them of it? In this way, I give myself permission to address my own issues rather than volunteering to take on everyone else's.

Holding space offers me an opportunity to support someone who is working through hard stuff without needing to physically or emotionally intervene. When others tell me that they are struggling with an issue, I keep their best interests in my thoughts and prayers. By doing so, I am energetically empowering them to be successful in their endeavor. Being a compassionate and loving presence is a kind and generous option, one that I now practice.

I'm seriously impressed by how many times my loved ones have been stepping up to the plate and rising to the occasion now that I've stopped making their issues my personal problem. Not to mention, they are proud of themselves for having accomplished this on their own. And I am proud of them as well! It's not easy!

Stress is not directly caused by our concern for others, our lifestyle of choice, or unanticipated circumstances that arise. Stress is a symptom of our emotional, mental, and physical responses to these situations. Every day we have endless opportunities to get angry, offended, or stressed out. When we indulge these negative emotions, we are giving these feelings power over our happiness—and ultimately over our health and well-being.

We can learn how to avoid letting issues push our buttons, especially those that are out of our control or are not our problems to begin with. With a little shift in perspective, we can gain valuable insight into what triggers us and find effective techniques that can assist us in learning how to modify our stress responses. Support is available from mentors, life coaches, ministers, counselors, or books by inspired authors. Embracing our reality differently can alleviate some of the anxious, depressing, or overwhelming feelings we have about our lives.

If changing how we react to our circumstances doesn't effectively reduce our level of stress, we can always consider altering our lifestyle or our approach to a specific situation. Leaving a harmful or oppressive environment is not always the easiest option, but it can break the cycle of abuse (self-abuse included). This is a liberating experience, often well worth the effort despite the apparent losses involved.

Joshua Kai advises, "Even the smallest shift in perspective can bring about the greatest healing." A paradigm shift – a fundamental change in our beliefs or our perceptions – naturally inspires a transformation in our approach to living life. Take my examples of the Fortress of Fear and the Love Cup. Those aha moments rewrote my life's script. It's hard to go back to a dysfunctional way of existing once we find an easier, more effective, and more satisfying way to experience our lives. Becoming conscious of how our lifestyles affect us is an essential step in bringing ourselves and our lives into harmony.

While society has lofty expectations of us, life is not obligated to give us what we've planned for or dreamed possible, so it pays to be realistic rather than idealistic. Sometimes simpler is better, especially when it allows us to manage our responsibilities, achieve our goals, and move closer to a state of inner peace.

Gerald Jampolsky encourages us when he says, "It's not the situation that's causing your stress, it's your thoughts, and you can change that right here and now. You can choose to be peaceful right here and now. Peace is a choice, and it has nothing to do with what other people do or think."

After an emotionally traumatic divorce followed by seven years of clinical depression, I realized that the only person who could put an end to my pathetic pity party was me. The antidepressants I was taking not only muted my depression but were inhibiting me from experiencing joy in my life. I knew I needed to wean off them. Then I stopped seeing my counselor/psychologist because she merely applauded my insight into my own dilemma rather than offering me any handy dandy tools for bouncing back from it.

While some people keep a diary or journal, I have collected quotes my entire life. I decided to take those that most inspired me, match them up with artwork or photography that resonates with each message, and post them in a blog which I named School of Fine Hearts. I committed to posting at least one of these pairings per day as my therapy. Within months, I was feeling like a new person. I've continued this inspirational practice for over six years. Others who follow these daily posts mention that they feel more positive about their lives as well.

Remember, you always have a choice, though you can't change what's going on around you until you change what's going on within you.

6

Being Healthy

*If it looks like a duck, walks like a duck and
quacks like a duck, it's probably a duck.—Jacques
de Vaucanson (as redefined by Louise Mita)*

My brother Paul taught me one of the greatest lessons. As
a brittle asthmatic child, he had multiple prescriptions
and over-the-counter medications to manage his
symptoms. I noticed that as an adult, he was no longer
taking medicine—not even a rescue inhaler. When I
asked what had changed, he explained that while most
people with allergies take medications to be able to live
with the irritants or life-threatening allergens in their
lives, he had opted for a more logical approach. He

chose to remove himself from any such environmental or emotional triggers.

He stays in his air-conditioned room when it's hot or smoggy. He avoids animals with fur or people who smoke. He only works as needed and on his own schedule. He doesn't enter into conflict or confrontation. He doesn't over-exert himself, and he eats only foods that agree with him. He has not needed asthma medication for almost forty years.

Making positive lifestyle changes can enable us to live a healthier life. Our bodies have a brilliant warning system that alerts us to what puts our well-being in danger. Red flags may include allergies, pain, anger, illness, injury, disease, anxiety, and depression. Do we really want to continue living or working in a toxic environment, especially if we know it's making us sick? Is taking medication to manage our symptoms a better solution than addressing what might be causing them? When I asked myself these questions, the answer to each was a resounding "No way!"

As a nurse, I observe that Western medicine and the pharmaceutical industry is dedicated to, and financially dependent upon, the perpetuation of persistent symptoms and chronic conditions. After specializing as a Legal Nurse Consultant for a couple of years and reviewing hundreds of toxic tort cases, I can assure you that pharmaceutical corporations are clearly aware that the side-effects of their medications can be worse than your initial symptoms ever were.

In fact, many physicians find it necessary to issue additional prescriptions to treat these undesirable side-effects. This adds up to more pills for their patients and more income for the drug manufacturers. The unfortunate truth is that the pharmaceutical industry makes so much money marketing these drugs, they can afford to settle lawsuits for deaths and disabilities related to their use. Let that sink in for a hot minute.

Optimal health comes when we have balance in our lives. As a practitioner, I have witnessed patients with stress-related symptoms improve dramatically when their energetic equilibrium is restored. The effects are often immediate, even if my patient is thousands of miles away. If you're wondering how this works, consider the following concept.

The composite of our physical anatomy consists of cells, made of molecules, made of atoms, made of nanoparticles, made of quantum energy. We are all essentially energy fields. People, prayers, colors, music/tones, crystals, aromas/fragrances, movements, foods, thoughts, words, emotions, songs, art, meditation, gravity, radiation, weather and frequencies affect us because everything is energy.

The trick is to know which of these influences throw our energetic balance off and which ones restore it. It may take years of energetic misalignment for severe symptoms or disease to arise, but once balance is restored, a sudden shift in one's condition is possible.

Health is a holistic phenomenon, and balance is essential for maintaining our natural state of well-being. Our optimal health is a reflection of the harmony of our body, mind, and spirit.

7

Being Resilient

The secret of life, though, is to fall seven times
and to get up eight times —Paulo Coelho

One of the things that sets America apart from the rest of the world is that we think we have it all. Yet amid the abundance, most people are struggling to find a life that fulfills them.

I believe that advancing our education beyond mandatory schooling really does make a difference—and not only because it helps us get a better-paying job. Through continuing education as well as international travel, I discovered that some of my former belief systems were cracked to the core. When exposed to the wisdom of great thinkers or civilizations, I am empowered to design new versions of my reality. These expanded beliefs allow me to increase my capacity to love myself and the world around me. Education inspires us to change at any age because learning is a lifelong process.

The key is to follow our hearts and our passions. If we know what makes our heart sing, we are invested in learning more about it. Our ideal career choice is doing what we love because then it's not like work—it's focused play. We are more awesome when we pour our passion into a purpose. Over time, we may even become the mentor who sets a new standard for excellence in our domain of amazingness.

People who are masters in their field of expertise have refused to give up despite epic failures—Mohammed Ali, Albert Einstein, Steve Jobs, Michael Jordan, Walt Disney, and J. K. Rowling come to mind. Difficulties that arise during the process of achieving our goals don't define us unless we choose to give up. Instead, they can strengthen our dedication to overcome any obstacles in our path. When the challenge gets tough and we get tired, we need to learn how to rest, not quit. It all begins with believing in ourselves. *A Course in Miracles* reminds us to "remember that you are deprived of nothing except by your own decisions."

Transformation is a constant in our lives. Growing from an infant to an elder is an evolutionary process involving adaptation to a multitude of experiences and environments. Ironically, change is the very thing that many people resist most. This resistance is often due to a desire to stay within our scope of familiarity (or comfort zone), even if we are putting ourselves at risk by choosing to remain there.

Some are intimidated by moving on to new experiences. For example, we may be reluctant to leave a job we dislike because we fear the steep learning curve or demands of a new one. Or we might be hesitant to leave a dysfunctional relationship because we'd rather have someone than no one, especially if we doubt our ability to survive on our own. We might think twice about moving to a new town or country because we don't know anyone there. For me, these jumping-off-a-cliff scenarios generate a level of anxiety that, in the past, might have easily tipped me into a state of panic. Now I'm more comfortable taking a leap of faith.

It helps to make the initial goals for any transition achievable ones. Change is a skill, and we can help ourselves succeed at change by acknowledging our small daily successes. This is the best way to ensure sustainability in our forward motion. Long-term plans are often risky, although the more realistic the goal, the less risk of failure.

I've never been much of a long-range planner but once chose to take a huge gamble and epically failed: I moved to Minnesota from Hawaii in the Winter of 2003 to be near my daughter Déja (and recover from my divorce). Although the Midwest was not on my dream itinerary, I found it lovely there (though very cold). Four years later, I opted to move to Southern California and was immediately hired to an administrative nursing position at a well-known medical center. I was unable to sell my home in Minnesota prior to the move due to the onslaught of the Recession of 2007, but since it was the nicest house in the neighborhood, I was confident that it would appeal to a savvy buyer with a sense of style. In retrospect, this turned out to be an unrealistic assumption given the economic atmosphere.

Two years later, I ended up losing both homes in foreclosure after unwittingly engaging in a loan modification scam. I was emotionally and financially devastated, vowing to never own a home again. Ultimately, it turned out to be an opportunity for me to reboot my life, but it took time and distance for me to appreciate that perspective.

With practice, taking small steps in a forward motion becomes easier. We become less focused on investigating which step is the right one, and we start learning to trust that the best one will present itself at exactly the perfect moment.

When I left Northern California to return to Southern California in 2016, I sublet my studio (for which I was paying over $1,500 per month). After opting to begin my Soul Journey, I knew I would not be able to afford that much rent on a retirement income, so I gave up the space. Almost immediately, a darling mother-in-law unit was offered to me in Southern California at a third of the cost. It seemed like a miracle! Or was it a confirmation that I was exactly where I should be?

Having faith in this process makes change easier and provides a solid foundation for profound growth to occur as we continue to move ahead on our paths. Which brings us to the Doors of Opportunity.

Most Doors of Opportunity don't automagically appear out of nowhere. Years ago, I realized that every day was an interview. People noticed that I went the extra mile in my job and wanted a role model for that kind of work ethic in their department. I made a conscious effort to be honest, efficient, punctual, curious, accountable, creative, and emotionally intelligent. I've had many doors open for me this way.

But I've also learned that you can't fake or force this. If the door doesn't open, it's probably not your door. I promise that if you are passionate, patient, and proactive, the right opportunity will present itself to you.

In 2011, I was sent to Northern California as a traveling Administrative Nursing Supervisor. After several months in this position, I was romanced by the Directors of three nursing departments within the hospital to take a permanent position as a Manager. I accepted the Emergency Department role, since that's where my training, experience, and expertise were the strongest. It was my Door of Opportunity.

Anticipating and allowing for change, as well as the willingness to get back up after things collapse all around us, are the hallmarks of resiliency. Though situations may fail us, we are not failures if we don't give up on ourselves. Sometimes failing allows us to reinvent ourselves and explore new opportunities. Sometimes it pays to be persistent in our passion. The best way to predict our future is to be willing to create and recreate it.

8

Being Detached

The easiest way to organize your stuff is to get rid of most of it.—*Joshua Fields Millburn & Ryan Nicodemus*

What was the hardest part of my process as I transitioned from my career to my Soul Journey? I know you didn't ask the question, but I'm going to share this bit of wisdom with you.

The hardest part of the process was detachment. While it's not easy to jettison our self-defeating beliefs or outdated concepts, let's chat for a moment about the stuff we've accumulated over the years. Some people are so attached to their material wealth that it becomes a significant part of their identity. I can let you in on a little secret: what you own is not who you are, even if the media leads you to believe it's so.

It's a painfully cathartic process to detach ourselves from our possessions, even if they don't fulfill a need - especially a gift from someone special. In truth, every item we own awakens a memory in us. So if we have the space, we usually choose to keep it—even if it ends up in a storage closet somewhere.

Those generations affected by the Great Depression tend to hold onto everything because they recall a time when they had nothing, not even food. For some of us, our material accumulation is inversely proportional to our sense of personal security. I know many people whose garages are so full of stuff that there's no room to park their cars. Few of them make use of the items that they've stashed away, but the idea of getting rid of them is generally nonnegotiable.

When I decided to scale down my living space to a small room, I nearly had a breakdown when my cousin Alix suggested that I choose only one of my four white shirts. I adored all of them, and each was different in its own unique way, but she was right. I finally picked out my very favorite white shirt and then asked her to leave so I could take a nap because that, and a dozen other similar decisions, had emotionally exhausted me. I was a basket case. And we were just going through my clothes!

In the end, I gave away three quarters of my clothing, shoes, purses, jewelry, and toiletries, and ninety-five percent of my furniture and household items (most were sold to my landlords to furnish the studio I was vacating). Everything that was left fit snugly into a large SUV. I cried that day.

I thought I was going to grieve this loss for months, but instead I experienced a sense of freedom—freedom from attachment, freedom from responsibility for the stuff I'd owned but never used. It was liberating, and I honestly don't miss any of it. The amazing thing is, I'm still surrounded by beautiful things and have exactly what I need to be healthy and happy.

And, by the way, the term *clutter* doesn't just apply to material things. It can relate to thoughts and feelings—especially resentment, guilt, fear, and worry. These pervasive concerns over past or future events distract us from being present. Detachment from these self-destructive emotions can also provide a sense of freedom.

An old Zen proverb teaches us, "Knowledge is learning something every day. Wisdom is letting go of something every day." There's no need to get rid of everything—just everything you no longer need.

9

Being Grateful

Acknowledging the good that you already have in your life is the foundation of all abundance.—*Eckhart Tolle*

While we're on the topic of detachment, gratitude is inextricably interwoven into this web. When I'm grateful for what I have, I don't need more. One of the easiest ways to boost the level of satisfaction with our lives is to keep a gratitude journal. I suggest that people start with a simple notebook in which they write a few things that they are grateful for each day. You don't need to have a notebook to do this - you can just think about a few *gratitudes* in the morning or at the end of the day.

My gratitudes, for example, might be simple:

- I slept like a rock for the first time this week.

- I remembered to set my alarm, so I wouldn't be late to my appointment.
- Thank God it didn't rain at the outdoor concert last night.

Or they are sometimes more specific:

- My daughter Déja asked me to watch her kids so she could have a break for a week, and this will give me time to hang out with my grandchildren.
- My friend Paul offered to take my household donations to the local shelter since my car was full of everything I was moving to Southern California.
- My son Jordan, who was run over by a car as a child, had nearly 100 percent recovery and now competes in long-distance bicycle races.

Engaging in this practice has a way of starting my day as if I'm looking through a gratitude filter. I just keep looking for more things to be grateful for instead of focusing on what isn't working out the way I'd hoped it would. Remember that what we concentrate on is where the energy of manifestation flows. In other words, we get what we wish for. Personally, I prefer to passionately propagate positivity. Elizabeth Gilbert says, "You have to participate relentlessly in the manifestation of your own blessings."

Gratitude has to do with appreciating what we have and accepting the way things are, as opposed to always wanting what we don't have. The latter has never worked for anyone, by the way, and it usually rolls out like this: We're not satisfied with what we have, so we want more. When we get it, we're still not satisfied with what we have, so we still want more. When we get it … well, you get it! This cycle of entitlement has no beginning and no end. It does not generate any deep or lasting sense of happiness.

Coming from a place of gratitude allows us to accept and appreciate what we already have and then, when something miraculously or through the fruits of our labor manifests, it feels like a gift, a reward for working hard for something or having faith that it would happen. This then increases our gratitude quotient, which mysteriously enables us to continue to manifest more amazingness while also generating a deep and lasting sense of happiness. It just keeps getting better and better.

Zig Ziglar explains, "Gratitude is the healthiest of all human emotions. The more you express gratitude for what you have, the more likely you will have even more to express gratitude for."

One of my most grateful moments came as I was catching an early flight home from Moloka'i in the summer of 1976. Five women, including my teenage cousin and me, made plans to hitchhike, backpack, and camp on Moloka'i over a weekend. Once there, we had a series of unusual experiences on our journeys to the Friendly Isle's valleys, waterfalls, and mountains. By *unusual,* I mean strong spirit energy: a self-proclaimed *Kahuna* (or Hawaiian medicine man) appeared at every destination we hiked to (though we never saw him on a trail); two huge rocks near one another clearly resembled a female and a male sex organ; and then, as we hiked along a barren trail through a mist-filled Ironwood forest, we were haunted by the lilting tone of an invisible nose-flute, only to discover that the path ended abruptly at a five-hundred-foot cliff.

After a long day of hiking, we finally found a spot to pitch our tents for the night, unaware that this area was *kapu* (forbidden). That night, under the full moon, we were attacked by Night Marchers—the ghosts of ancient Hawaiian warriors. It's a long story, but I will tell you that all five of us were huddled together in one tent praying, chanting mantras, singing, and anything else we could think of that would inspire God, angels, saints, prophets, or loving spirit guides to rescue us from our terrifying audiovisual nightmare.

Out of nowhere (because we *were* in the middle of nowhere), we saw headlights nearing our campsite. As if in answer to our prayers, a young farmer had meandered up to the area, dared by two local women at a bar to see if he had the guts to drive up to this sacred hot spot on a full moon. We ran out of the tent and begged him to take us out of the forest— anywhere else but there! Bobby kindly helped us load our stuff into the back of his pickup truck and drove us quite a distance to his house in the middle of an expansive pineapple plantation. He invited us inside his home and generously offered his living room floor for us to spread out our sleeping bags.

Over two hours later, we were awakened by the sound of distant chanting. Looking out the window into the darkness, we saw torches rhythmically marching toward his house. The Night Marchers had followed us untold miles from our campsite. His home had been blessed long ago by a Hawaiian priest and thankfully, they could not touch us. Still, none of us dared sleep, including Bobby. When the sun came up in the morning, we were *so* ready to leave that island! Bobby offered to drop us at the airport to await the first flight back to Oahu.

Grateful doesn't even begin to touch how I felt as that plane left the Moloka'i Airport (and I still say a blessing for Bobby each day). It was an experience I will never forget!

Whether we keep a gratitude journal, think of gratitudes, express our appreciation verbally or write thank-you notes, being grateful enables us to be happier and healthier, improves our relationships, and makes life more rewarding for us and everyone around us.

10

Being Honest

Everything that irritates us about others can lead us to an understanding of ourselves. —*Carl Jung*

I've always been reclusive in my personal life, mainly because I never had much privacy, especially as a young single mom. Taking time out from the chaos of my world allows me to recharge my life-force battery, so I intentionally design my personal spaces as sacred sanctuaries that are both relaxing and restorative. In the past, time spent with friends often resembled a group therapy session (which seemed more like work than relaxation), but that's what friends are for, right?

I realized that because I'm an empath, a nurse, and a mother, I naturally attracted people who were seeking consolation and approval. This provided me with endless opportunities to be a compassionate, loving, and kind person. Obviously, I had a caretaker personality and was someone who needed to feel needed. Of course, I also had friends who loved and nurtured me.

Recently, it started bothering me to hear some of my friends repeat various versions of why their life sucks. Sure, I'd been that whiny person in the past: feeling taken for granted, overwhelmed, overworked, overtired, and, during menopause, overheated. In those good old days, I actively participated in our misery-loves-company conversations, even though I would often end up feeling emotionally deflated rather than energetically pumped up. But now, well, I'm just not into it. Why?

I had to take a long hard look at this. It only started annoying me after I transformed my life into a positive one that no longer sucked. Could it be that since I started to value my own worth and have more control over my life, I find it harder to hang around people who choose to mire themselves in their own negativity? Maybe so. My sincere desire to be a good friend and support others in moving out of their suffering prompted me to start taking a different approach in these conversations.

Presently, when I speak with friends who are inclined to incessantly complain or assume the victim role in every story, I listen compassionately without validating or engaging in their soap opera. I might gently challenge them, if I sense that they are totally unaware of being stuck in their not-so-mellow-drama, by saying, "You know you have a choice, right?", or "If you hate your situation so much, is there anything you could possibly change that could make it better?"

I asked one friend to imagine her never-ending issues with her adult son as a virtual basketball game. By engaging in his dysfunctional behavior, she was enabling that behavior to continue. She'd been playing the game according to his rules. He expected her to buy him every expensive thing he wanted or needed. Every time she bought him what he asked for, he won the game. Once she decided to stop buying him everything he asked for, she took possession of the ball and control of the game. She is no longer a victim.

The truth is, if I didn't love these friends so much, I wouldn't be taking the time and energy to be a mirror, reflecting their issues back to them. I'd have walked away from those relationships a long time ago. This straightforward approach appears to be beneficial for some of them, and it's certainly working for me. Some of these friends have made positive changes in their lives, and the others ... well, they don't talk to me anymore.

Honesty. It's a win-win!

11

Being Fulfilled

People who wonder if their glass is half-empty or half-full are missing the point. The glass is refillable. —*Unknown*

It's challenging work, growing up and taking responsibility, especially when the unexpected happens. For example, my young adult life was regularly interrupted by unplanned pregnancies. After being told that I would never be able to have children, I turned out to be one of a handful of women for whom every form of birth control known to science had zero effect. It was a blessing and a curse—mostly a blessing.

I left home and got a job at age seventeen, immediately after graduating high school. My father died when I was eighteen, and two years later (once his will was released from probate court), I began to receive a small distribution of funds each month. I was incredibly fortunate. This stipend allowed me to attend college in Southern California, and it continued to be a source of financial support after I moved to Hawaii with my infant son in 1974.

When I was twenty-one years old and living on the island of Oahu, a friend named Sandy (she'd been with me and my cousin on Moloka'i) asked if I would accompany her on a visit to see a fortune-teller in Kaimuki. *Sure!* I thought. *Why not?* We walked up to what looked like a haunted house, both a little nervous about what awaited us inside. An elderly Asian woman greeted us at the door. She told fortunes by reading playing cards and palms. I remember her inspecting the side of my hand and reporting that I would be having five children. *You must be out of your mind* was my visceral response.

I spent the next fourteen years trying to prove that little old lady wrong. As skeptical as I had been about her prophecy, and as diligent as I was with every form of birth control I'd been prescribed, she was right all along!

I enjoyed being a full-time mother, but as my family and the local economy both flourished, I started working a variety of small jobs to stay afloat. Despite my extraordinary predisposition to pregnancy, I hadn't been as successful in love. As a result, I was a single parent throughout most of these years. After my fifth child was born (the surviving twin of a post-tubal-ligation pregnancy), I decided to return to college to earn my nursing degree and RN license.

I became an Emergency Nurse to support my family, make a difference in people's lives, and serve my community. This was a dream job. It fulfilled my personal needs as well as my desire to be engaged in humanitarian service by being able to practice kindness and compassion almost daily. I also had plenty of time to spend with my family, which included weekends at the beach and holiday camping adventures. Those years make up a large part of my kids' best memories.

Because I was a people person, a role model, and a natural leader, I was offered multiple promotions. As happy as I was in my Emergency Department Charge Nurse job, I was flattered by offers to be promoted to increasingly more powerful positions. Ultimately, I ended up in roles that were more focused on bureaucracy than patient care. It later dawned on me that I'd lost touch with the very reason I became a nurse in the first place.

Though my career became stressful and consuming, I continued to be admired and respected in my various roles. I kept pushing harder for what was needed and worked longer hours to get the work done, usually without the benefit of the resources that were promised along the way. Finally I realized that there was a limit to what I could do, and I had reached it.

It's common in our society to focus incessantly on what we have yet to achieve and continually push ourselves in the more-is-better direction. A healthier approach is to acknowledge all that we have accomplished in life and applaud those moments when we shined our brightest. Again, this is about being fulfilled by what we have or what we're doing rather than desiring more.

Rest, recovery, and reflection are also essential components of success—at any stage of the game. Why work so hard if we can't appreciate the fruits of our labor? Creating a sustainable lifestyle is the key to a healthy and gratifying one. As you can see, I found this out the hard way.

The Dalai Lama, when asked what surprised him most about humanity, answered, "Man. Because he sacrifices his health in order to make money. Then he sacrifices money to recuperate his health. And then he is so anxious about the future that he does not enjoy the present—the result being that he does not live in the present or the future—he lives as if he is never going to die, and then dies having never really lived."

I recently chose a simpler life—one more aligned with my passion—in order to save my life. What I've learned is that rather than aspiring to be like role models, often steering ourselves away from our unique purpose, we can inspire ourselves to be soul models, in alignment with our essential reason for being in this present existence (as well as in all conceivable lives in past and future timelines). In this way, we are not only enriching our lives, we're fulfilling our destinies.

12

Being Joy

The very life within you is longing to be joyful because joyfulness is the nature of the source of creation.—
Jaggi Vasudev

Do you ever wonder why we're here? I did. I have spent years pondering and researching this very topic. Want to know what I've discovered so far? I believe that our purpose in life is *being joy!* So how do we get in touch with joy? The first step is to find out what makes us happy. The more we discover about what makes us smile versus what stresses us out, the easier it is to make adjustments that lead us toward a state of joy.

I loved my role as an Emergency Nurse. As a single mom with five kids, I enjoyed the gratification of feeling valued by grown-ups (my peers and patients)—and, I'll admit it, going to work was a little time-out from my parenting responsibilities. Once I climbed up the career ladder, though, I found that the demands and expectations of bureaucracy not only kept me further than I wanted to be from my family but also generated toxic stress that spilled over into my private life.

Toward the end of my nursing career, I was lonely, depressed, exhausted, and barely surviving. I knew I had to get out. Ironically, my peers, family members, and the local Social Security representative couldn't understand why I would give up financial security when I could still work for at least eight more years before retiring with a hefty pension. But joy had suddenly become a priority in my life, and my health and happiness were priceless.

Tom Bodett shares this wisdom: "They say a person just needs three things to be truly happy in this world: someone to love, something to do, and something to hope for." I believe there is a lack of joy in present-day America because so many are too busy to devote time to their families and friends; are laboring in positions that they don't love; or have lost hope. These are all contributing factors to our country's escalating rates of mental health issues, addiction, and suicide.

The truth is that we, as a humanity, are all connected. We flourish with the love and support of family and friends, whereas we fail to thrive when isolated. By the way, the friends we hang out with in person and our virtual friends on social media are not the same. When we find ourselves in situations that separate us from this connectedness, especially from loving relationships, we begin to lose joy and hope. We feel depressed and abandoned, like we're dog-paddling to keep our heads above a rising tide.

The more honest we can be about what makes us happy and what doesn't, the easier it is to create a life that we love. There may be sacrifices to make, such as stepping down from a career role to one with less responsibility, moving to another state to be able to buy a more affordable home, or walking away from an abusive relationship or environment. I've experienced every one of these.

One way to create joy in our lives is to take a stand for what's right and demand to get what we deserve (or what makes more sense for the collective cause), with an emphasis on transforming the situation into one more aligned with integrity. I've done this in many hospitals across the country, as the current corporate model of patient care tends to forget about caring for the patient and I am a relentless advocate for patient rights. I have always chosen to be part of the solution rather than participate in perpetuating the problem. It feels good to do the right thing.

Sometimes it helps to take a trip to someplace far from home to get a fresh perspective on life. Immersing ourselves in another country's lifestyle and exposing ourselves to their cultural priorities, however briefly, has a profound effect. Whether it's a deluxe package tour, a hitchhiking/hostel pilgrimage, a backpacking/camping adventure, or a volunteer exchange program, the result is the same. The experience itself is far more valuable than the cost of the journey. Traveling has a way of gently humbling me into a state of gratitude, redefining my beliefs, and connecting me to nature and the brother/sisterhood of humanity. As David Mitchell writes in *Cloud Atlas*, "Travel far enough, you meet yourself."

And then there are some who willingly sacrifice their personal preferences to do what's best for their loved ones. This makes them happy because they know they're providing a better life for their family. People who work on cruise ships, for example, are away from home for nine months out of the year, but they're generating an income they could never dream of making in their homeland. These moms and dads hang out with their kids via computer, and for them, it's good enough. Their unconventional choice creates joy in a unique way.

We are the only ones who can choose our options (once we stop letting others choose for us), and there are always options when we are living our lives consciously. Joy comes when we're in alignment with ourselves and our purpose. It is our most natural state of being.

13

Being Complete

Almost everything will work again if you unplug it for a few minutes, including you.—Anne Lamott

Life is not a race to see who can get to the end fastest. It's an opportunity to savor each moment and make it last as long as possible. If you are chronically too busy for your loved ones or always rushing to your next destination, why not slow down, take a step back, and reassess your life? It's not up to anyone else but me to have a life that I choose for myself, and it's no one else's fault if it's not looking like I want it to.

Why not make our dreams come true? I spent some time as a Hospice nurse, so I'm not just being cliché when I say that no one arriving at the end of life regrets not having worked longer or harder. Patients of all ages have shared with me that they wished they had fulfilled their childhood fantasies; taken those trips to faraway places; told their partner or children "I love you" more often; managed to have more balance in their life; or shown up for their kids more. Most of all, they wished they had been true to themselves and followed their heart.

Stop and take a deep breath! When things look like they're out of control or falling apart, maybe that particular series of events needed to happen so things could finally fall into place. This is exactly the time when the Doors of Opportunity open. But if we're too busy picking up all those pieces of our formerly broken lives and mourning them, we won't notice that there's an open door with our name on it.

Instead of panicking, be patient and allow the next step to unfold. The best choices are the ones we offer to our inner guidance, allowing time and space for the perfect opportunity to present itself. They are not the ones that we settle for out of desperation, that we intellectualize incessantly over (pros/cons), or for which we compete relentlessly.

Last year, my nursing license was up for renewal. As I mentioned earlier, I'd been on my Soul Journey and not actively working as a nurse. To renew my license, I am first required to complete thirty hours of continuing education units (CEUs), so I signed up for an online course on "Death and Dying with Dignity." The course study guide was immense, immaculately researched, and deeply philosophical. For weeks, I agonized over having to study the huge volume of material (I think I managed to get through the first chapter).

I was running out of time and on the verge of panic. I considered just letting my RN license lapse or even applying for inactive status (no CEUs required for that). Then it occurred to me that, as a former Hospice nurse, I should know this stuff already. Right? I took the test without even studying and passed with a score of eight-five percent. (Please note: I'm not recommending that people don't study for tests. In this case, I was already trained in the material being tested.)

When we navigate through life in this flow, we find that things get easier, our lives take on more positivity, we finally get to spend quality time with our loved ones, we have less stress, and we feel happier, healthier, and more complete. It's a dance of self-love.

Chris Assaad asks us to "Close your eyes and imagine the best version of you possible. That's who you really are; let go of any part of you that doesn't believe it." Go ahead, try it!

I care more about my relationship with my inner self than ever before. If my life is not in alignment with myself, then I have nothing to offer anyone else. All these years later, I've learned that we must first love ourselves!

There are five Cs in life: courage, conscious, choice, chance, and change. We must have the courage to make a conscious choice to take a chance if we want to see a change. Once we stop feeling guilty about putting our own needs first, we can make a fresh start. Yes, we do get second chances to have a complete life makeover. I've started over and reinvented my life more times than I care to remember. In truth, we can have as many do-overs as we need to be not merely satisfied but ecstatic about our lives.

14

Being Human

I am a human being, not a human doing.—*Kurt Vonnegut, Jr.*

When I have an experience that resonates with me (causing goose bumps or little electric zaps), I am excited and encouraged. I know that this is right for me. When I am in a situation where I feel tense or resistant (or vaguely sick to my stomach), I know that what is happening is somehow wrong for me. It's a pretty simple algorithm to follow: *Do this. Don't do that.*

I once had neighbors who were a sweet and beautiful family. Our kids played together all the time in Waimanalo. The parents were constantly inviting me to come to their church, but I always politely declined.

NANI LAWRENCE, RN, MSN, CIQM

Finally, they mentioned that their church was having an Easter sunrise service on the beach and there would be a potluck meal afterward. Would I come?

Well, beach and food? Maybe so! I hesitantly agreed to go. By the way, I'd never been to church before, but I had traveled around the world and met some of the kindest people from a variety of different countries, cultures, and religions. I thought of myself as open-minded and nonjudgmental, and yet the closer we got to the beach, the more I wished I'd driven myself.

About halfway through the service, the pastor became very animated and began to wave his hands, exclaiming that anyone who didn't adhere to the church's standards would burn in Hell. Thinking of all the lovely people I'd met around the world, I was suddenly overwhelmed by nausea and spent the remainder of the service in the beach's public restroom hurling into a sandy toilet. No potluck feast for me.

Obviously, his truth wasn't my truth, and that's okay. I'm not in a position to judge anyone else's spirituality, on any level. I *am* entitled to my own beliefs, which are subject to change as I mature—whenever aha moments encourage me to shift my perspective and expand my reality. Being in alignment with our higher self or our higher purpose doesn't require an advanced technological degree. It's not rocket science. It requires that we be present, tune in to our inner awareness, and pay attention to our physical or emotional cues to have a sense of what's best for us.

Ironically, this is where intellectualizing has a way of flushing our instincts right down the drain. Being defensive or in denial because the intuitive path seems unreasonable or uncomfortable doesn't serve us. Sure, the signs we receive do not always look like guideposts for the Yellow Brick Road, but we need to trust that we don't need a wizard to discover who we are and what we need to thrive. We just need to wake up, be present, and pay attention to the signs that each moment brings us. Some of us aren't there yet, but better late than never!

To show up as our best selves in our family, our workplace, and our community, we must first meet our own basic needs. By making ourselves a priority, we manage all our responsibilities more efficiently and with less stress. When I choose myself first, I'm not being selfish—I'm ensuring that I will be able to give one hundred percent to my chosen endeavors. We can't pour anything from an empty cup. We need to ful*fill* our needs first, much like my overflowing Love Cup.

Being in the moment, without regretting the past or fearing the future, makes this process easier.

Jane Goodall once said, "You cannot get through a single day without making an impact on the world around you. What you do makes a difference, and you have to decide what kind of difference you want to make."

Remember, our purpose in life is not winning competitions or amassing material wealth (although there's no reason not to be awesome). It's *being joy*! It's being a fluid component of positive change. It's connecting with the oneness of humanity, the laws of nature, and the rhythm of the universe. If we want to leave our children a legacy, let's make it one of peace.

In my humble opinion, anything that generates divisiveness is an obstacle to peace. This includes war, religion, politics, corporate models, social injustice, competitive sports, etc. It is only through inclusiveness that we will be able to foster an environment worthy of future generations. Being authentic, grateful, and loving—as well as accepting and respectful of our collective differences—is a good place to start. A. D. Williams invites us to "Imagine what seven billion human beings could accomplish if we all loved and respected each other. Imagine."

We can only accomplish this by being fearless. I won't lie—it's challenging to detach from old patterns, programs, and things. But soon we realize that our lives get easier and more meaningful the more we practice letting go. Those beliefs, stories, possessions, expectations, relationships, habits, and careers that we've worked so hard to sustain or conform to, but which haven't contributed in a meaningful way to our joyfulness, may be worth discarding. We might consider unpacking our proverbial bags and seeing how much lighter our load can be.

Awakening, or en*lighten*ment, is an awareness that inspires positive transformation. I believe that we will be able to alter the current state of our world as more of us awaken, embrace these *sacred secrets*, and commit ourselves to a purpose that goes beyond the egocentric life we've been living but not loving. World peace can only be achieved by first experiencing inner peace or peace of mind. Once we accomplish this, we will find ourselves *living in a state of grace*. As Taoist Master Wang Fou put it, "If you want to awaken all of humanity, then awaken yourself. If you want to eliminate all the suffering in the world, then eliminate all that is dark and negative in yourself. Truly, the greatest gift you have to give is that of your own self-transformation."

In social dynamics, *critical mass* is a sufficient number of believers in a concept (the square root of one percent of the population, to be more specific) to cause the belief to become self-sustaining and support exponential growth.

The term has its origin in nuclear physics, where it refers to the amount of a substance needed to sustain a nuclear chain reaction.

In the 21st century, a good example of this phenomenon is the smartphone. Nowadays, most of us can't even imagine how we survived without one. These mobile devices allow us access to sources of information that have both exposed and promoted some of the greatest mass deceptions in our history. They connect humanity beyond borders while at the same time virtually disconnecting us from some of our most intimate relationships. The world is a different place because of these phones.

What if we were to reach a point of *critical mass* in our efforts to promote the concepts of world peace and basic human and animal rights? There is a strong possibility that this is already in the process of happening. Are you with me on this? It's kind of a big deal!

I hope to inspire you to consider the value that any one of the *sacred secrets* may have for you. If you apply these simple principles and sense how dramatically the energy shifts in your own life, please pass them along to others who may benefit from them as well. By becoming mindful of our choices, as well as nurturing and encouraging others in this direction, we can ignite a movement of oneness, collectively transforming our aha moments into a tsunami of aloha (peace, love, kindness, generosity).

My personal goal in sharing these *sacred secrets* is that more of us will find joy in the current chaos and be better prepared for an uncertain future. I believe that, as the currently corrupt world paradigm becomes dismantled (wait for it – it's happening), together we can and will generate a positive force that shall envelop this planet in goodness and joy! We can only do this by being united in love and compassion. Please join me!

Aloha ke akua!
(Breath of Life—Love of God)

ADDENDUM
Quote References

1. *Maya Angelou:* "**Having courage does not mean that we are unafraid.** *Having courage* and showing *courage mean we* face our fears. *We* are able to say, 'I *have* fallen, but I will get up.'"

2. *Les Brown:* "**Too many of us are not living our dreams, because we are living our fears.** Decide to become fearless. Face the thing you fear the most. You are stronger than you give yourself credit for. If you can laugh at it. You can move past it. You have the ability to do more than you have ever hoped, imagined or dreamed. You have greatness within you!"

3. *Shannon L. Alder:* "The most glorious moment you will ever experience in your life is when you look back and see how God was protecting you all this time."

4. *Sadhguru:* "Love is a process of inclusion. Once I include you as a part of me, I will be to you just the way I am to myself."

5. *Gerald Jampolsky:* "If you don't forgive your mother and father, all of your partners in relationships will be versions of your mother and father." (related to me by Andrea Smith from a personal conversation with Jerry Jampolsky)

6. *Unknown:* "Never assume that loud is strong and quiet is weak." (extensive search made for author)

7. *His Holiness the 14ᵗʰ Dalai Lama:* "When you talk, you are only repeating what you already know. But if you listen, you may learn something new." (this is also credited to author J.P. McEvoy, though no one is sure which of the two laureates quoted it first)

8. *Mark Batterson:* "You're always one decision away from a totally different life." (from his book, *All In*, published by Zondervan)

9. *Joshua Kai:* "Even the smallest shift in perspective can bring about the greatest healing." (from his book, *The Quantum Prayer*, published by Waldorf Publishing)

10. *Gerald Jampolsky:* "It's not the situation that's causing your stress, it's your thoughts, and you can change that right here and now. You can choose to be peaceful right here and now. Peace is a choice, and it has nothing to do with what other people do or think."

11. *Jacques de Vaucanson:* "If it looks like a duck, walks like a duck, and quacks like a duck, it's probably a duck." (this quote is used frequently by my teacher, Louise Mita, to describe the obvious)

12. *Paulo Coelho:* "The secret of life, though, is to fall seven times and to get up eight times." (from his book, *The Alchemist*, published by HarperCollins)

13. *A Course in Miracles:* "Remember that you are deprived of nothing except by your own decisions." (page 48, scribed by Helen Schucman, published by the Foundation for Inner Peace)

14. *Joshua Fields Millburn & Ryan Nicodemus:* "The easiest way to organize your stuff is to get rid of most of it." (from their book, *Minimalism: Living a Meaningful Life,* published by Mins Publishing)

15. *Zen Proverb:* "Knowledge is learning something every day. Wisdom is letting go of something every day."

16. *Eckhart Tolle:* "Acknowledging the good that you already have in your life is the foundation of all abundance." (from his book, *A New Earth: Awakening to Your Life's Purpose,* published by Plume)

17. *Elizabeth Gilbert:* "Happiness is the consequence of personal effort. You fight for it, strive for it, insist upon it, and sometimes even travel around the world looking for it. **You have to participate**

relentlessly in the manifestations of your own blessings. And once you have achieved a state of happiness, you must never become lax about maintaining it. You must make a mighty effort to keep swimming upward into that happiness forever, to stay afloat on top of it." (from her book, *Eat, Pray, Love*, published by Penguin Books)

18. *Zig Ziglar:* "Gratitude is the healthiest of all human emotions. The more you express gratitude for what you have, the more likely you will have even more to express gratitude for." (as quoted by his son, Tom Ziglar, in the book, *Mastering the Power of Your Emotions*, by Elisha O. Ogbonna, published by Friesen Press)

19. *Carl Jung:* "Everything that irritates us about others can lead us to an understanding of ourselves." (from his book, *Memories, Dreams, Reflections*, published by Vintage Publishing)

20. *Unknown:* "People who wonder if their glass is half-empty or half-full are missing the point.

The glass is refillable." (extensive search made for author)

21. *His Holiness the 14th Dalai Lama:* "Man. Because he sacrifices his health in order to make money. Then he sacrifices money to recuperate his health. And then he is so anxious about the future that he does not enjoy the present – the result being that he does not live in the present or the future – he lives as if he is never going to die, then dies having never really lived." (in response to a question posed to him about what surprised him most about humanity)

22. *Jaggi Vasudev:* "The very life within you is longing to be joyful because joyfulness is the nature of the source of creation."

23. *Tom Bodett:* "They say a person just needs three things to be truly happy in this world: someone to love, something to do, and something to hope for." (from his book, *As Far As You Can Go Without a Passport: The View From the End of the Road*, published by Perseus Books)

24. *David Mitchell:* "Travel far enough, you meet yourself." (from his book, *Cloud Atlas*, published by Random House)

25. *Anne Lamott:* "Almost everything will work again if you unplug it for a few minutes, including you." (from her TED Talk, *12 Truths I Learned from Life and Writing*)

26. *Chris Assaad:* "Close your eyes and imagine the best version of you possible. That's who you really are; let go of any part of you that doesn't believe it."

27. *Kurt Vonnegut, Jr.:* "I am a human being, not a human doing." (this quote is also attributed to Wayne Dyer)

28. *Jane Goodall:* "You cannot get through a single day without making an impact on the world around you. What you do makes a difference, and you have to decide what kind of difference you want to make."

29. *A.D. Williams:* "Imagine what seven billion human beings could accomplish if we all loved and respected each other. Imagine."

30. *Wang Fou:* "If you want to awaken all of humanity, then awaken yourself. If you want to eliminate all the suffering in the world, then eliminate all that is dark and negative in yourself. Truly, the greatest gift you have to give is that of your own self-transformation." (from the book, *Hua Hu Ching*, written by Taoist Master Wang Fou and translated by Brian Walker – credit for this quote is most often incorrectly given to Lao Tzu and his Tao Te Ching)

ABOUT THE AUTHOR

Nani Lawrence, RN, MSN, CIQM

Nani Lawrence is a registered nurse whose successful career includes roles in Midwifery, Emergency Medicine, Disaster Medical Response, Legal Nurse Consulting, Hospice Care, Education, Advocacy, and Leadership. She has forty years of experience in the field of energetic realignment, with certifications in Jin Shin Jyutsu, Biofeedback Technology, and Integrative Quantum Medicine™ (IQM). She currently practices as a Certified

Practitioner and Instructor of IQM, inspiring others to discover their optimal health, truth and joy.

Having dedicated her life's work to the integration and alignment of universal energies to perpetuate healing, empowerment, and the oneness of humanity, Nani donates time and energy to network with light workers around the world to protect our precious planet so that its beauty and magic may be preserved for future generations.

She is the founder of School of Fine Hearts™, first created in 2012 to share her innovative self-help practice for successfully combating situational depression. School of Fine Hearts™ (www.schooloffinehearts.com) currently showcases Nani's energy work, focusing on the Integrative Quantum Medicine™ technique developed by her teacher and mentor, Louise Mita.

Nani presently resides in Ojai, California, having spent most of her adult life in Hawaii. She has five grown children and several grandchildren, some of whom share her passion for the art of energetic healing.

CPSIA information can be obtained
at www.ICGtesting.com
Printed in the USA
FSHW011315051118
53562FS

9 781504 397087